MW01601468

The Easter Jokes for Kids Book

Over 250 Silly, Goofy, Knock Knock and Funny Holiday Jokes and Riddles Perfect for Friends and Family at Any Easter Party

DL Digital Entertainment
MADE TO ENTERTAIN

DL Digital Entertainment

THE EASTER JOKS FOR KIDS BOOK

TABLE OF CONTENTS

INTRODUCTION

We would like to personally thank you for taking the time to purchase our book *The Easter Jokes for Kids Book.* We have spent countless hours putting together only the best and most interesting Easter themed jokes and riddles for you, the kids and the entire family to enjoy! You can expect to find 200+ different jokes, riddles and brain teasers ranging from easy, hard, funny, silly and goofy Easter themed entertainment. These jokes, riddles and brain teasers are guaranteed to make you think hard and have all kinds of fun while doing so.

We are happy to present this book in the form of audio so you can listen at ease and with friends and family so everyone can join in on the fun. The joes, riddles, brain teasers through-out this book will be read out at a comfortable pace to make sure everyone can follow along without an issue. After each has been read out twice, you will be given 12 seconds to come up with an answer. Trust us, 12 seconds is enough time and it will give you plenty enough time to think and come up with an answer.

The Easter Jokes for Kids Book is very versatile thanks to being in audio format! Use it on your own before bed, with friends at a get together, with family at the dinner table or camping with relatives; the possibilities with it are endless. Be creative and utilize it to its full potential!

WHY JOKES?

This ultimate assortment of jokes for kids, family and friends will not only make you laugh but do so in a fun and interactive way. Jokes have been around since the dawn of time and have many other benefits such as:

-Confidence Boosting: *With so many kids and people in general struggling with self-confidence in our day and age, listening and interacting with these jokes in a safe environment with family and friends gives them the opportunity to comfortably say answers and repeat hilarious jokes, giving them the ability to not be afraid to express themselves.*

-Relieve Stress: *Jokes help in relieving your anger, depression, tension and stress and make you feel light and irritation free. It also improves the mood by reducing anxiety and fear. Laughter increases heart rate and blood pressure, both of which cools down your stress response.*

*-**Improved Bonding:** The Easter Jokes for Kids Book is one of the best ways for friends and family to spend time with each other and build positive, healthy relationships through laughter and participation when listening to the jokes and trying to answer the questioning ones.*

*-**Personal Health:** Jokes make us laugh and impacts the body in a very positive way. When you start to laugh, it not only lightens your body but also induces many physical changes in it as well. Not only that, but funny jokes boost up the human immune system by increasing infection fighting antibodies.*

*-**Reduce Boredom:** Having an audiobook such as The Easter Jokes for Kids Book gives you the ability to have fun and entertainment on demand. Since we provide it in audiobook form, it gives you the opportunity to utilize it in any situation!*

*-**Develop Humor:** Jokes sharpen your sensibilities and tune our capabilities. It improves your personality by bringing*

out your lighter side. Humor also allows people to express their feelings without any hesitation.

Now, that's enough talking. Are you ready to get started with *The Easter Jokes for Kids Book.*

Awesome! Let's Begin.

EASTER JOKES!

1. Q. Why shouldn't you tell an Easter egg a good joke?

   A. It might crack up!

2. Q. What did one colored egg say to the other?

   A. Heard any good yolks lately?

3. Q. How many chocolate bunnies can you put into an empty Easter basket?

A. Only one because after that, it's not

empty!

4. Q. What kind of beans never grow in a garden?

A. Jelly beans!

5. Q. How does the Easter bunny stay in shape?

A. Lots of eggs-ercise!

6. Q. What do you call a dumb bunny?

A. A hare brain.

7. Q. What's the best way to catch a unique rabbit?

A. Unique up on him.

8. Q. How do you catch a tame rabbit?

   A. Tame way, unique up on it.

9. Q. What happened when the Easter Bunny met

   the rabbit of his dreams?

   A. They lived hoppily ever after!

10. Q. Why can't a rabbit's nose be twelve inches

    long?

    A. Because then it would be a foot.

11. Q. How can you tell which rabbits are the oldest in

    a group?

    A. Just look for the gray hares.

12. Q. What do you call a line of rabbits walking

backwards?

    A.   A receding hareline.

13. Q. How do you know carrots are good for your

eyes?

    A.   Have you ever seen a rabbit with glasses?

14. Q. What do you call a rabbit who tells jokes?

    A.   A funny bunny.

15. Q. What is a rabbit's favorite dance?

    A.   The Bunny Hop.

16. Q. What do you call a rabbit with fleas?

    A.   Bugs Bunny.

17. Q. How do rabbits say good-bye to carrots?

    A.   It's been nice gnawing you!

18. Q: How does a rabbit make gold soup?

    A: He begins with 24 carrots.

19. Q: What do you get when you cross a bunny with

    a spider?

    A: A harenet.

20. Q. Why does the Easter bunny have a shiny nose?

    A.   His powder puff is on the wrong end.

21. Q. What is the difference between a crazy bunny and a counterfeit banknote?

    A. One is bad money and the other is a mad bunny!

22. Q. Why is a bunny the luckiest animal in the world?

    A. It has four rabbits' feet.

23. Q. What do you get when you cross a bunny with an onion?

    A. A bunion.

24. Q: When is an elephant like the Easter Bunny?

A: When he's wearing his cute little Easter Bunny suit.

25. Q: What do you call a chocolate Easter bunny that was out in the sun too long?

A: A runny bunny.

26. Q: Why couldn't the rabbit fly home for Easter?

A: He didn't have the hare fare.

27. Q: Why did the rabbit cross the road?

A: Because the chicken had his Easter eggs.

28. Q: Where do Easter bunnies dance?

A: At the basketball.

29. Once there were two chocolate bunnies and one

    had their ear bit off.

    One said, "Happy Easter."

    "Huh?" Said the other.

30. Christmas does come before Easter in one place—

    but where?

    The dictionary!

31. What's the best way to make Easter easier?

    Put an "i" where the "t" is.

32. What do you get if you give an Easter Bunny a pair of socks?

A sock hop!

33. Q. What do you get if you pour hot water down a rabbit hole?

A. Hot cross bunnies!

34. Q. What do you call a rabbit with fleas?

A. Bugs Bunny!

35. Q. How did the soggy Easter Bunny dry himself?

A. With a hare-dryer!

36. Q. What did the rabbit say to the carrot?

A.   It's been nice gnawing you!

37. Q. How did the Easter Bunny rate the Easter

parade?

A.   He said it was eggs-cellent!

38. Q. How does the Easter Bunny travel?

A.   By hare-plane!

39. Q. How does the Easter Bunny stay fit?

A.   Eggs-ercise and hare-robics!

40. Why do we paint Easter eggs?

Because it's easier than trying to wallpaper them!

41. What do you call ten rabbits marching backwards?

A receding hareline.

42. Why was the Easter Bunny so upset?

He was having a bad hare day!

43. Where does a bunny go when it dies?

To the HARE-after.

44. Why didn't the bunny hop?

No bunny knows.

45. What happened when the Easter Bunny stuck his

head in the fan?

It took EARS off his life.

46. What is the Easter Bunny's favorite state capital?

Albunny, New York.

47. What did the Easter chick say when it hatched out

of the shell?

"What an egg-sperience."

48. What college did the Easter Bunny graduate from?

John HOPkins.

49. How do you catch the Easter Bunny?

Hide in the bushes and make a noise like a carrot!

50. What's the difference between the Easter Bunny

    and a lumberjack?

    One chews and hops, the other hews and chops.

51. What is the Easter Bunny's favorite sport?

    Basket-ball, of course...

52. What day does an Easter egg hate the most?

    Fry-day.

53. How can you tell where the Easter Bunny left his

    treasure?

    Eggs marks the spot.

54. What kind of stories does the Easter Bunny like

best?

Ones with hoppy endings.

55. How does the Easter Bunny keep his fur neat?

With a hare brush.

56. What did the Easter Bunny do after his wedding?

He went on his bunnymoon.

57. How many eggs can you fit in an empty Easter

basket?

One. After that, the basket isn't empty anymore.

58. What's the best way to send a letter to the Easter

Bunny?

By hare mail.

59. What kind of bunny can't hop?

A chocolate bunny.

60. How does the Easter Bunny feel after Easter?

Eggs-hausted.

61. How do you know the Easter Bunny is really

smart?

Because he's an egghead.

62. What happened to the Easter Bunny when he

misbehaved at school?

He was eggspelled.

63. What kind of jewelry does the Easter Bunny wear?

A: 14 carrot gold!

64. Q: What do you call a forgetful rabbit?

A: A hare-brain!

65. Q: Where does the Easter Bunny get his eggs?

A: From an egg plant!

66. Q: What kind of beans grow in the Easter Bunny's

garden?

A: Jelly beans!

67. Q: What did the father egg do when the mother

egg told him a joke?

A: He cracked up!

68. Q: What do you get if you cross a bee and a

bunny?

A: A honey bunny!

69. Q: How does the Easter Bunny keep his fur shiny?

A: With hare spray!

70. Q: What do you get if you cross an elephant with a

rabbit?

A: An elephant who never forgets to eat his

carrots!

71. Q: Why did the Easter Bunny hide?

A: Because he was a little chicken!

72. Q: What happened to the egg when he was

tickled?

A: He cracked up!

73. Q: What do you call a rabbit with the sniffles?

A: A runny bunny!

74. Q: How do you know the Easter Bunny liked his

trip?

A: Because he said it was egg-cellent!

75. Q: How does the Easter Bunny paint all those

Easter Eggs?

A: He hires Santa's elves to help during their off

season!

76. Q: What is the Easter Bunny's favorite dance?

A: The bunny hop!

77. Q: Why is the bunny the luckiest animal?

A: Because they have four rabbits feet!

78. Q: What you get if you cross a rabbit with an

insect?

A: Bugs Bunny!

79. What does the Easter Bunny say when it does a

burp?

A: Eggs-cuse me!

80. Q: Why don't you see dinosaurs at Easter?

A: Because they are eggs-tinct!

81. Q: Why did the Easter Bunny cross the road?

A: No bunny knows!

82. Q: What do you call an Easter Egg from Outer space?

A: An Egg-stra-terrestrial!

83. What did the eggs do when the light turned green?

A: They egg-cellerated!

84. Q: Who is the Easter Bunny's favorite movie actor?

A: Rabbit Downey Jr.!

85. Q: What would you get if you crossed the Easter Bunny with a stressed person?

A: An Easter basket case!

86. Q: Why did the Easter Bunny have to fire the

    duck?

    A: Because he kept quacking all the eggs!

87. Q: Why does Peter Cottontail hop down the

    bunny trail?

    A: Because his parents wouldn't let him borrow

    the car!

88. Q: What do you call rabbits that marched in a long

    sweltering Easter parade?

    A: Hot, cross bunnies!

89. Q: How can you tell which rabbits are the oldest in

    a group?

A: Just look for the grey hares!

90. Q: Where do Easter Bunnies go for new tails?

A: To the re-tail store!

91. Q: What do you call a sleeping egg?

A: Egg-zosted!

92. Q: How do you know when you're eating rabbit

stew?

A: When it has hares in it!

93. Q: What does a rooster say to a hen he likes?

A: Your one hot chick!

94. Q: How does an Easter chicken bake a cake?

A: From scratch!

95. Q: Why are people always tired in April?

A: Because they've just finished a March!

96. Q: What kind of book does a rabbit like at

bedtime?

A: One with a hoppy ending

97. Q: What kind of stories are the Easter Bunny's

favorite?

A: Bunny Tales!

98. Q: Where did the Easter Bunny learn how to ski?

A: The bunny hill.

99. Q: What looks like half an Easter Bunny?

A: The other half!

100. Q: How does the Easter Bunny's day

always end?

A: With a Y.

101. Q: What kind of car does the Easter Bunny

drive?

A: A hop rod.

102.   Q: Which side of the Easter Bunny has the

most fur?

A: The outside.

103.   Q: What do you say to the Easter Bunny

on his birthday?

A: Hoppy birthday!

104.   Q. What does the Easter Rabbit get for

every basket he makes?

A.   Two points, unless he's past the 3-point

line.

105.   Q. Why can't the Easter Bunny's ear be twelve inches long?

A. Because then it would be a foot.

106.   Q: What game does the Easter Bunny like to play on his driveway?

A: Hopscotch.

107.   Q. How can you tell the Easter Bunny was a boyscout?

A. He helps little old bunnies cross the street.

108.   Q: Why did the Easter Bunny throw the clock out the window?

A: He wanted to see time fly.

109.   Q: Where does the Easter Bunny go for

pancakces?

A: IHOP (Internation House of Pancakes)

110.   Q: What does the Easter Bunny pant next

to the green beans in his garden?

A: Jelly beans.

111.   Q: What do you get if you cross Winnie

the Pooh and the Easter Bunny?

A: A honey bunny.

112.   Q. What did the Easter Bunny put a

dictionary in his pants?

A.   He wanted to be a smarty pants.

113.   Q: Why did the Easter Bunny eat the gold

ring?

A: He was told it was 18 carrot.

114.   Q: What did one Easter egg say to the

other Easter egg?

A: Want to hear a funny yolk?

115.   Q: How does the Easter Bunny get his

cardio workout?

A: By doing hareobics.

116.		Q. What do you call a bunny with a large

brain?

	A.	Egghead!

117.		Q. What did the bunny want to do when

he grew up?

	A.	Join the Hare Force.

118.		Q. How does the Easter Bunny say Happy

Easter?

	A.	Hoppy Easter!

119.		Q. What grows between your nose and

chin?

A.   Tulips (Two Lips).

120.   What's the difference between a

counterfeit dollar bill and a crazy rabbit?

One is bad money, the other is a mad bunny!

121.   Q: What the Easter Bunny's favorite dance

move?

A: The bunny hop.

122.   Q: What sport are the eggs good at?

A: Running

123.		Where did the Easter Bunny learn how to

ski?

The bunny hill

124.		How does the Easter Bunny travel on

vacation?

On hare planes

125.		How do rabbits stay cool during the

summer?

With hare conditioning

126.		How can you tell which rabbits are the

oldest in a group?

Just look for the gray hares

127.   What does a bunny rabbit do in the rain?

Get wet

128.   Where does Dracula keep his Easter

candy?

In his Easter casket

129.   What do you call the Easter Bunny on the

day after Easter?

Tired

130.   What do you get when you cross a bunny

with an onion?

A bunion

131.   Knock, knock

Who's there?

Mora

Mora who?

Mora chocolate bunnies

132.   Knock, knock

Who's there?

Howie

Howie who?

Howie gonna get all the Easter eggs?

133.   Knock, knock!

Who's there?

Boo.

Boo, who?

Don't cry, the Easter Bunnies will come back next year

134.   Knock, knock!

Who's there?

Dewey.

Dewey who?

Dewey have to listen to any more ether bunny jokes?

135.   Knock, knock!

Who's there?

Donna.

Donna who?

Donna want to decorate some eggs?

136.   Knock, knock!

Who's there?

Esther.

Esther who?

Esther Easter Bunny coming?

137.   Knock, knock!

Who's there?

Justin.

Justin who?

Justin time to do the Bunny Hop.

138.   Knock, knock!

Who's there?

Howard.

Howard who?

Howard you like to find an Easter egg?

139.   Knock, knock!

Who's there?

Alma.

Alma who?

Alma Easter eggs are gone. Can I have one of

yours?

140.   Knock Knock!

Who's there?

Sherwood.

Sherwood who?

Sherwood like to have an Easter basket

141.   Knock Knock!

Who's there?

Carrie

Carrie who?

Carrie my Easter basket please, it's too heavy

142.   Knock Knock!

Who's there?

Donut.

Donut who?

Donut forget to say Happy Easter!

143.   Knock Knock!

Who's there?

Hans.

Hans who?

Hans off my Easter candy!

144.   Knock Knock!

Who's there?

Tommy.

Tommy who?

Tommy aches from eating too many Easter jelly

beans.

145.   What do you get when you cross a rabbit

with an oyster?

The oyster bunny

146.   Why couldn't the Easter egg family watch

T.V.?

Because their cable was scrambled

147.   What do you call a mischievous egg?

A practical yolker

148.   What's pink, has five toes, and is carried

by the Easter Bunny?

His lucky people's foot

149.   What is the Easter Bunny's favourite state

capital?

Albunny, New York

150.   What do you need if your chocolate eggs

mysteriously disappear?

An eggsplanation

151.   Why was the father Easter egg so strict?

He was hard-boiled

152.   What would you get if you crossed the

Easter Bunny with a famous French general?

Napoleon Bunnyparte!

153.   What type of movie is about water fowl?

A duckumentary

154.   What do ducks have for lunch?

Soup and quackers

155.	Why is the letter A like a flower?

A bee comes after it

156.	Knock, knock.

Who's there?

Arthur.

Arthur who?

Arthur any more Easter eggs to find?

157.	Knock, knock.

Who's there?

Chuck.

Chuck who?

Chuckolate Easter bunnies are my favorite.

158.	Knock, Knock

Who's there?

Eggs.

Eggs Who?

Eggs-cited for the Easter Bunny!

159.   Knock, knock.

Who's there?

Harvey.

Harvey who?

Harvey happy Easter.

160.   Knock, knock.

Who's there?

Wendy.

Wendy who?

Wendy Easter Bunny going to come?

161.   Knock Knock

Who's there?

Some bunny

Some bunny who?

Some bunny has been eating my Easter candy!

162.   Knock, Knock

Who's there

Easter

Easter Who?

Easter Bunny!

163.   Knock, Knock?

Who's there?

Ana

Ana who?

Ana-other Easter Bunny!

164.   Knock, knock

Who's there?

Easter

Easter who?

The Easter Bunny!

165.   Knock knock

Who's there?

More

More who?

More Easter bunnies.

166.   Knock knock

Who's there?

Even more

Even more who?

Even more Easter bunnies.

167.   Knock knock

Who's there?

Car

Car who?

Car come and run over the Easter bunnies.

168.   Knock, knock

Who's there?

Some bunny

Some bunny who?

The Easter Bunny!

169.   Knock, knock

Who's there?

Easter Egg

Easter Egg who?

The Easter Bunny!

170.   Knock, knock!

Who's there?

Heidi.

Heidi who?

Heidi the eggs around the house.

171.   Knock, knock!

Who's there?

Alma.

Alma who?

Alma Easter candy is gone!

172.   Knock, knock!

Who's there?

Police.

Police who?

Police hurry up and find all the eggs.

173.   Knock, knock!

Who's there?

Boo.

Boo who?

Don't cry, Easter will be back next year!

174.   Knock, knock!

Who's there?

Butcher.

Butcher who?

Butcher eggs in one basket!

EASTER RIDDLES!

175.   In March or April

These things do abound

A certain bunny

Leaves these on the ground

Answer - Easter Egg

176.   Sometimes these are hollow

And have chocolate inside

Other times they're real

And you paint their outside

Answer - Easter Egg

177.   When you wake up on Easter Day

It's always time to hunt for these

Look for these ovals high and low

So climb up and get on your knees

Answer - Easter Egg

178.   What Am I?

I'm colorful but I'm not a rainbow

I'm hunted for but I'm not an animal

I sometimes contain chocolate but I'm not an

advent calendar

I have a shell but I'm not a crab

I'm sometimes painted but I'm not hung on a wall

I'm left by a bunny but I'm not the remains of a

carrot

Answer - Easter Egg

179.   He goes hopping around

Leaving some eggs behind

So that on Easter Day

You will have treats to find

Answer - Easter Bunny

180.   When it is Easter

I go hopping around

Leaving lots of eggs

Which then need to be found

Answer - Easter Bunny

181.   I'm an animal

And I like to hop

I have Easter eggs

That I like to drop

Answer - Easter Bunny

182.   I'm something hopping round dropping

eggs on the ground

What Am I?

Answer - Easter Bunny

183.   I drop things but I'm not clumsy

Answer - Easter Bunny

184.   I like to hop but I don't have a pogo stick

Answer - Easter Bunny

185.   I'm an animal but I'm not a dog

Answer - Easter Bunny

186.   I leave eggs behind but I'm not a chicken

Answer - Easter Bunny

187.   I come out at Easter but I'm not a

Cadbury's Creme Egg

Answer - Easter Bunny

188.   You would have seen three of these

On the Calvary hillside

One of which carried Jesus

On Good Friday when he died

Answer - cross

189.   It can look like a T

It can look like an X

They can be found on chains

Hung around people's necks

Answer - cross

190.   If you encounter a vampire

Make sure you remember this rule

You can ward them off with garlic

As well as this Christian symbol

Answer - cross

191.   On Calvary

There were three, not six

It's also known

As a crucifix

Answer - cross

192.   I look like the letter t and am a symbol of

Christianity

Answer - cross

193.   Q. Why didn't the bunny hop?

A.   No bunny knows.

194.   Q. How did the rabbit cross the road?

A.   He hopped he could.

195.   Q. How do you kill a unique rabbit?

A.   You neak up on it.

196.   Q. Why do rabbits eat carrots?

A.   Because they don't want to be

nearsighted!

197.   Q. How does a rabbit throw a tantrum?

A.   He gets hopping mad.

198.   Q. What do you get if you cross a bee and

a bunny?

A.   A honey bunny!

199.   Q. What stories does the Easter Bunny like

best?

A.   The ones with happy eggings!

200.   Q. How did the Easter Bunny rate his

favourite restaurant?

        A.   Egg-cellent!

201.   Q. What kind of bunny can't hop?

        A.   Ones made of chocolate!

CONCLUSION

Wow! You made it through all 200 of the hilarious Easter themed jokes this book.... How did they go? Did you have fun? These jokes have all been hand picked in order to make you laugh like there's no tomorrow! We hope you enjoyed going through them and they created some great memories between you, your friends and your family.

Once again, we would like to thank you for reading our book *The Easter Jokes for Kids Book* and we can't wait to hear what you thought about it. If you enjoyed listening to this book, please don't forget to leave a review and let us know exactly how much you loved it. Reviews mean the world to us and help us continue to create books just like this one for years to come.

Happy Easter!

DL Digital Entertainment

Made in the USA
Monee, IL
07 April 2020

25237487R00042